Bones of Stardust

Mishi Ashraf

MAPLE
PUBLISHERS

Bones of Stardust

Author: Mishi Ashraf

Copyright © Mishi Ashraf (2024)

The right of Mishi Ashraf to be identified as author of this work has been asserted by the author in accordance with section 77 and 78 of the Copyright, Designs and Patents Act 1988.

First Published in 2024

ISBN 978-1-83538-275-2 (Paperback)
        978-1-83538-276-9 (E-Book)

Cover Design and Book Layout by:
        White Magic Studios
        www.whitemagicstudios.co.uk

Published by:
        Maple Publishers
        Fairbourne Drive, Atterbury,
        Milton Keynes,
        MK10 9RG, UK
        www.maplepublishers.com

Tell us about the book

This book is a captivating tapestry of emotions, weaving together threads of love, pain, resilience, empowerment, and self-discovery in a breathtaking display of poetic artistry.

With eloquent language and poignant imagery, each poem invites readers on a transformative journey, guiding them through the depths of human experience. From the raw vulnerability of heartbreak to the triumphant resilience of the human spirit, these verses resonate deeply, leaving a permanent mark on the soul after the pages have been turned.

Dedication

This book is dedicated to all who have dared to embrace their scars and find poetry in their journey. To people who inspired these poems—thank you for being part of my journey. Your presence has left a mark on my heart, and to my dear **MOTHER**, whose love and support have been my guiding light, like stars twinkling in the night, and to the dreamers, the seekers, and the wanderers of the soul. May these verses be a refuge for your heart.

she is the tapestry
of stardust,
with glory echoing
in her bones
and grace cascading
through the depths
of her marrow.

—bones don't lie

water your brain and heart.
pour scents and serenity into it.
let daisies, lilies, and sunflowers
bloom on your skin,
and let the butterflies chant
above this radiant garden.

—*blossom*

i have embraced womanhood
with pride for so long.
what haven't i borne?
from a cracked heart to a soul tormented,
i journeyed through mountains of pain,
and i deserve a trophy engraved on it:

"the iron woman".

our bones were hungry, feeling frail,
our lips were thirsty, dry as shale,
our eyes were tired, seeking rest,
our hearts were sore, minds stressed,

when we first met, our worlds aligned,
in shared weariness, our souls combined.

—*meeting of souls*

i am not one but various:

the whisper of the wind,
and the roar of the ocean.
i am the silence between heartbeats,
and the laughter among the stars.
i am the doorway to realms
of joy and beyond.
i am infinitely infinite,
without a bound.

—*boundless*

i set all the butterflies
free that were
murmuring in me,
to let them choose the colours
they like,
the flowers they want,
and the flavours they love.

—*freedom*

she secludes
herself
from the world,
that can't see.

galaxies glow
in her eyes
and mountains
of glee.

—*solitude*

at this time of year,
when everything is
vibrant and full of
warmth,

what is not so
temperate is your
heart, cold to the
core heart.

so frosty and snowy,
i can see through you.
nothing there reminds
me of June.

—cold-hearted

in my bones,
you found the sun's
warm embrace,
the moon's gentle glow,
and stars' glorious grace.
yet, you turned away,
leaving me to wonder why.
did you realise?
you lost the entire sky.

—*loss*

those eyes of hers
were full of dreams,
with a purple moon and
orange sunbeams.

those eyes of hers are
now like deep wells,
full of raging thunders
and empty shells.

—transformation

before you land into my poems,
some of them are honey, some poison.

you can sip my words woven within lines,

the choice is yours,
thrive or resign, between rhymes.

—choose

i had the last drop
of rain dripping down
from my eyelash,

falling on my lips
to remove the dirt
of vicious thunders,

and waiting for a miracle
to come down
and hug me on God's

—*B E H A L F*

she will keep
singing the truth
until death
swallows her.

—*unafraid*

she treaded through
blind alleys in search of
love amidst wild waves.

until the truth whispered to her:

only she can fill
her pores with the
warmth she truly craves.

—*whispers of truth*

i poured my heart into the ink,
in the silent whispers
of my verses,
in the gallery of my thoughts,
in every metaphor and simile,
i have touched, hugged, and loved
you through my poetry.

—embrace

she did not
let wounds
dwindle her
spark.
she danced
with scars
and turned
those wounds
into soothing
melodies of
guitars.

—perfectionist

she is the poetry,
not everyone
can comprehend
and absorb.

　　　—*beyond*

even pain
could not make
the flame of her heart
dead.

she turned her scars
into stars
and let her light
spread.

—*scars into stars*

she turned grey ashes
into silver stars,
and turned into pearls
her dark scars.
she candled the darkness
world left her in,
and broke those cages time
kept her in.
she penned down her pain
and let it scream,
and wrapped in reality
her every dream.
she adorned her cheeks with
bright smiles,
and cheerfully chanted her songs
of trials.
she turned her wounds into
tamed rhymes,
and turned those rhymes into
sweet chimes.
she embraced her wounds
and danced with scars,
she turned cold ashes into
twinkling stars.

—*transformation*

she knows how to
guard her throne.

she is the master of
several arts,

and one of them is
surviving alone.

—survivor

if it's keeping
your soul starved
and heart parched,
it is not love.
true love fills your pores
with calmness,
quenches your thirst,
and tranquilizes your soul.

—fulfillment

only real love can
sprout happiness on a wounded heart.

—*cure*

you should not visit me
in a heavy cloak of ego.
meet me when you are
like the sky, so naked
and indigo.

come to me
when night is drowsy
and the moon sighs.
hold me gently
and let me melt
in your eyes.

—embrace in the night

i no longer allow
my heart to dance
to false promises' tune,

nor do i let my ears
drink delicious lies too soon,

now, i don't let my soul plunge
into deep and dark pits of

G L O O M

do not say yes to a maybe.

in realm of verse,
you rise high,

beyond adjectives,
where dreams fly.

—ineffable

a pinch of warmth
and a few ounces of love
can make us feel healed.

—*dose*

if hearts were meant
to be sliced,

they would have grown
on trees, not inside.

—hearts are human

be a shooting star
and soon,
you will find your
moon.

—*belief*

dear women,
radiant and bold,
you should celebrate your
presence, and let it unfold.

you have come this far
through your persistence,
and moved the mountains
of resistance.

you are living your dreams
and casting bright beams,
you have wings to fly,
and you can hug the blue sky.

you are where you wanted to be,
dear women,
your triumphs universe can see.

—*celebration*

in dreams bleeding,
with heart torn,

through bloodshed,
she walked alone.

—*warrior*

pain is my muse.

let them steal
some of your light.

it might help them
to candle the dark corners
of their heart.

—radiance

she sings her gloom,
sitting near a silent, drowsy river,
from midnight to dawn.

—grief

in a world
full of thunder,
be the
SUNSHINE

sometimes, you don't
choose the pain.
sometimes, pain finds you
and make your body its home,
slowly settling,
into the cracks of your heart
and seeping into your soul.

—*uninvited*

she hates
cages or anything that
binds,

restricting her
freedom and confining
her mind.

—*free*

a bunch
of tears it gives me
every time i let it foot
on my heart.

—*past*

she will never settle for a cage.

she is more
than
eyes can see
and minds
can envisage.

—*magic*

i don't regret
loving you profoundly.
i am a woman with atoms
made of love and
and fidelity.
you should be repentant for
leaving my heart bruised
with injuries.
i swear, my body still carries
that debris.

—*heartache*

it's not easy to
turn your heartbreaks
into poems,
sighs into melodies,
and pain into songs.

—*art*

she helped me regrow my wings
after they were completely splintered,
letting me dive into skies
vast and azure tinted.
she broke all the cages
that could have seized my flights,
and cut the chains
that could have bound me tight.
she taught me to fight against my fears,
she showed me how to drink my tears.
she gripped my hand through
joy and dismay,
shaping who i am today.

—*mother*

walk into my poems
and live there,

until you find
your truth laid bare.

—*discovery*

sun kisses her
in the morning,
moon envelopes her at night,
and stars wave to her at dawn.
cosmos, it seems,
is captivated by her love.

—*admiration*

she will choose
to fly
even if it's
with just one wing.

—*always*

she has
snatched light
from the throat of darkness
many times,
and she is not afraid to dive
into dark
and famished nights.

—*courageous*

her eyes, her face
her voice, her brain,
and her heart —
God must surely be rejoicing,
for crafting such a celestial

MASTERPIECE.

scars on her heart
are a tale of battles
she fought in silence.

—footprints

what brings you pleasure brings you pain.

all of us choose
ways to survive,
and some of us
choose to write.

—*escape*

if they can't
handle your magic,
the lack is
in their craft.
you should not
water yourself down
and fit to
their standards.

—*be you*

her heart is gold,
her mind is light,
and her soul is pure
camphor.

—*radiant*

i bleed for days,
and my atoms are at war with each other.
i feel blue and cry over my pillow.
i eat like a voracious horse,
and my body feels tender and sore.
i cook, clean, work and pen poems.
i survive this every month
and do not give up.

convince me, how am i not a wonder
woman?

—*phenomenal*

playing hopscotch
atop the sky she longs,

amidst the stars, the moon
and all beyond.

—*dream*

where were you?
when she needed you
the most?
unable to hold back her tears,
her heart bled
and soul cracked.
where were you then?
when she needed you
to erase the pain from her lips.
where were you then?
when she needed one hug of yours
to pacify her.
and now you return,
when she has collected her pieces
and rebuilt herself.
she no longer needs you
can't you see?
your presence is worthless,
like debris.

—*too late*

do you wonder
where i live?
a small room,
spacious enough for two of us.
books in one corner,
and some scents in the other.
a lot of silence, and three mirrors.
here, i live
with my lonesomeness.

—*abode*

between dusk and dawn,
somewhere, you will find
HOPE

letting go
is more peaceful
than holding on

—*sometimes*

you claimed to be a provider,
yet all you gave her was
infidelity, loneliness, and chaos
swirling in every trace.

—deception

she might forgive
the damage you did to her,
but she will never
let you step into the alley again
that leads to her heart.

—*banished*

let your heart
be healed
let this soreness
go away,
let that wound
get dried.

do not squeeze it,
do not drain,
do not peck at it
again and again.

—*let it heal*

it might seem like
a tragedy now,
but some goodbyes are blessings,
some breakups help you
grow better,
some disconnections
reconnect you with yourself,
and let you breathe freely.

—*liberty*

do not
kiss loneliness.
that mouth
is sharp like
a wild weed.

it will cut your lips
with its cruel teeth
and make your
tongue bleed.

—ruthless

only your
arms made
me feel
like home.

—*solace*

one morning,
i hope i to wake up with no regrets.
all sweet and sour
memories will vanish.

one night, i hope all pain will be gone,
and dusk will turn into dawn.

—*optimistic*

you awoke
the little girl inside me
with sheer playfulness.

—*magician*

when spring arrives
we will sit on the brink
of silver streams,
holding each other's hands
in golden sunbeams.

we will be lying under the
naked, dark blue sky.
we will laugh, clap,
dance, and cry.

we will get lost
in the purple valleys.
we will play hide-and-seek
in narrow alleys.

when spring arrives,
we will be together again.
we will twirl and swirl
in the silver rain.

—*reunion*

wind whispers,
loneliness murmurs,
and the fear of losing you
pierces my mind.
night sings, my heart trembles,
and soul feels numb.

—echos

she has been
carrying the sun in one
and rain in the other hand
for ages.

—*burdens*

she fell
for his wrinkles,
grey hair, ripened love
and everything
beyond.

   —obsession

you calmed down
the unsettling noise
inside me.

—God

do not sow love on a heart
that you have stepped on
and know is dark and barren.

—*fruitless*

i will ask you
to disguise yourself
as a woman for a day,
walk in bazaar and face
those hungry
and lustful gazes.
then tell me how it feels
to be a woman?

—*challenge*

i do dishes and laundry
i cook food and clean the house,
i raise kids and write poems too.
and all i want is some orange sun,
a gentle breeze
and a few drops of silver rain,
to soothe my sore soul
and calm my weary brain.

—respite

your lap is such a peaceful shelter.

—mother

half love, half heart,
and half of everything,
crumbs in a fancy bowl
you bring.

have you forgotten?
i fed your bones with love
when they shivered, deprived
of warmth.

i let you sip from my
soul's deep well
when weariness consumed
you.

do i deserve half love?
do i deserve a half heart?
do i deserve to be left
unattended, unhealed,
and unloved?

  —confrontation

she squeezed herself
in the dim corner of her room
enveloped tip to toe in the dark gloom.
grief and fear consumed her.
in her heart, they stirred a blur.
though time passes and wounds slowly heal,
your essence lingers,
a presence she cannot conceal,
in her bones, in the whispers of her soul,
bits and pieces of you, forever whole.

—*farewell*

my heart craves you, but my mind craves peace.

—*conflict*

he cleaved his ego's head
there,
and wept upon my bosom
bare,
like an infant, his tears did flow,
that night, forgetting
he was a man, i know.

—*dissolved*

our eyes were blushing,
and hearts were sweating,
when we cuddled,
under the flock of drowsy stars.

— *warmth*

she is searching
for some warmth
and light
in a sunless land.

—*deprived*

can you
disrobe
my heart
and love it
tip-to-toe
like a
wild wolf?

—*plead*

sore eyes, tired hair,
and pale smiles.
it looks like she has not been
in tender hands.

—*neglected*

i had the most cherishing time
while being in your arms,
a million mornings squeezed
into a dozen dawns.
when my lips were engaged
in deep conversations with your lips,
and words trembled
on the skinny brims of sweet sips,
and my soul was free
for a few moments from every pain,
and my heart twirled
like the velvety tunes of a violin.

—*euphoria*

i have kissed my wounds
and hugged my scars.
i have welcomed pain as a 'guest'
and i have bestowed compassion
upon everything.
with soul wounded
and a burdened chest.

—*resilience*

i long for solace,
crave freedom's embrace,
with a sky wide open
to find my space.

to breathe, to fly and freely roam,
underneath the vast sky,
i will find my home.

—*quest*

she wants
her skin
to be touched
to be read, smelt
and felt.

—urge

i have the power to reject them too,
not to shatter their pride,
but to save my shine.
why does this stir storms in their eyes?
why can't i transform too?
why can't it be a norm too?

—roar

my eyes make them
feel intimidated—
fearless, deep, and invulnerable eyes.
eyes that only eat
bitter truths and stay wise.
eyes that will never taste
tempting lies.

—*daring*

my mother and i
both dealt with my heartbreaks.
i shed tears, and she became my solace,
and each droplet of sorrow gently wiped
away.

i spoke, and she listened,
embracing every syllable.
she has always been there for me,
during highs and lows,
cradling me through storms and woes.

—*bond*

i want Asia
where choosing
not to marry
being divorced,
widowed,
or childless
is not a taboo.

— *urge*

whenever i miss you,
i close my eyes
and say your name.
do you know
what i see?
the empty night
is filled with the fragrance
of your memories,
and my soul whispers,
"Rest in peace".

—*father*

i have embraced every side of myself:

the joyous, the saddest the exquisite,
the wildest, the radiant, and the darkest.

with boundless love and generosity,
i have forgiven myself completely.

and i have decided to treat myself with grace,
care and love for the rest of my life.

—*affirmation*

in the tapestry of your life,
one relationship, one stumble
and one fall— none define you.

you are infinitely infinite,
and nothing can shrink
your immensity.

    —*immeasurable*

my mother
is my true inspiration.
she taught me
how to weave through
a pitch-black tunnel
with hope and prayer.

—*wisdom*

every time i look
at the sky it winks at me.
the stars smile, and the moon
sends hope.

—*connection*

you too saw me as
a flesh and bone.
you too beheld
just what you desired,
ignoring the depths within:
my heart's whispered melody,
and my soul's hidden light.

—*blind*

you promised
you will always be there for me if i need you.
where are you?
where is your love?
where is your madness?
i desperately crave it.
my heart is ravenous, and my soul parched.
can you give one morsel of your love
to my heart and satiate its appetite?
can you give one drop of your madness to
my soul
and quench its thirst tonight?

—desperate

she buried her heart
under her pillow
and wept like a little girl.

—*farewell*

scars, when dealt artistically,
transform into stars.

—*artistry*

the road outside
is lush green
except for one alley,
lean and dim,
a fainting plant
with dead white
flowers on it.
and an ivy vine
with holes-ridden
leaves draping over a
cracked wall.
in the midst stands
a small windowless house
where she resides.

—*encaged*

i have always been an admirer of stars.

we all have
hungry moons
within us
that we
forgot to feed.

—*unfed*

there
is nothing
more unsettled

than

being neither here
nor there.

—*immigrants*

in minds fed on mediocrity,
i will linger,
as a mystery unresolved.

—*enigma*

in you, i found my moon.

i extend my deepest gratitude
to all women, past and present,
born in ages long gone,
who bravely battled for my existence.

to those who nurtured me,
my mother, grandmother,
my father's mother, and more.
and to those who championed my rights.

accept my heartfelt appreciation,
for being phenomenally phenomenal,
in every step, every stride,
your legacy remains eternal.

—*acknowledgment*

Milton Keynes UK
Ingram Content Group UK Ltd.
UKHW030751121124
451094UK00013B/770

9 781835 382752